Unco
the Past

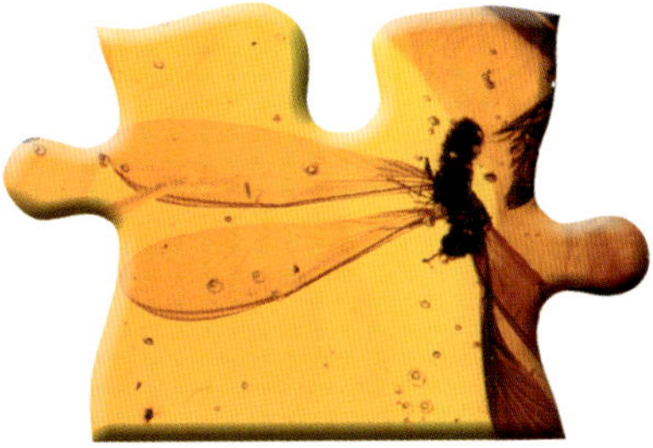

by Sharon Richards

HOUGHTON MIFFLIN HARCOURT
School Publishers

ILLUSTRATION CREDIT: Patti Isaaks

PHOTOGRAPHY CREDITS: Cover Howard Grey/Getty Images. 1 Howard Grey/Getty Images. 2 © Lowell Georgia/CORBIS. 3 (r) © Kevin Schafer/CORBIS. (magnifying glass) © Thomas Brummett. 4 (r) © Naturfoto Honal/CORBIS. (magnifying glass) © Thomas Brummett. 5 © Louie Psihoyos/CORBIS. 6 Associated Press. 7 (l) D. Erickson, University of Michigan. (r) Earl Scott/Photo Researchers, Inc. 8 © Bob Krist/Corbis. (magnifying glass) © Thomas Brummett. 9 © Staffan Widstrand/CORBIS. 10 © Vienna Report Agency/Sygma/Corbis. 11 © Jochen Tack/Alamy. 12 Howard Grey/Getty Images. 13 © Louie Psihoyos/Corbis. 14 Larry Miller/Photo Researchers, Inc. (magnifying glass) © Thomas Brummett.

Printed in China

ISBN-13: 978-0-547-02088-4
ISBN-10: 0-547-02088-0

9 10 11 0940 18 17 16 15 14 13
4500416904

Have you ever wondered what life on Earth was like long ago? Some scientists ask this question all the time. They find answers to it, too. They do this by looking for clues.

This scientist is digging for clues with a brush.

This is a fossil of a turtle from long ago.

Clues in the Ground

Some clues are found in the ground. They are called fossils. A fossil is what is left of an animal or plant long after it dies. Fossils can form in different ways.

This fossil shows what a fish from long ago looked like.

Most fossils form when an animal dies and gets covered with dirt. After thousands and thousands of years, the dirt turns to rock. A picture of the animal is left in the rock.

Other fossils form when animal bones get covered with dirt. Over a very long time, the bones turn into stone. These fossils can stay in the ground for millions of years.

Scientists can put together dinosaur fossils to show what the animal looked like.

Many animal bones were found in this famous tar pit in Los Angeles, California.

Clues in Tar Pits

Fossils in rock aren't the only clues to the past. Other clues have been found in pools of tar called tar pits. Tar is a kind of oil that bubbles out of the ground. Long ago, animals got stuck in the sticky tar pits and died.

The tar covered the animal bones and kept them from falling apart. Over time, the bones became hard fossils. Some of these bones are from animals that no longer live on Earth.

The tar pits have bones of animals that no longer live such as mastodons and saber-toothed tigers.

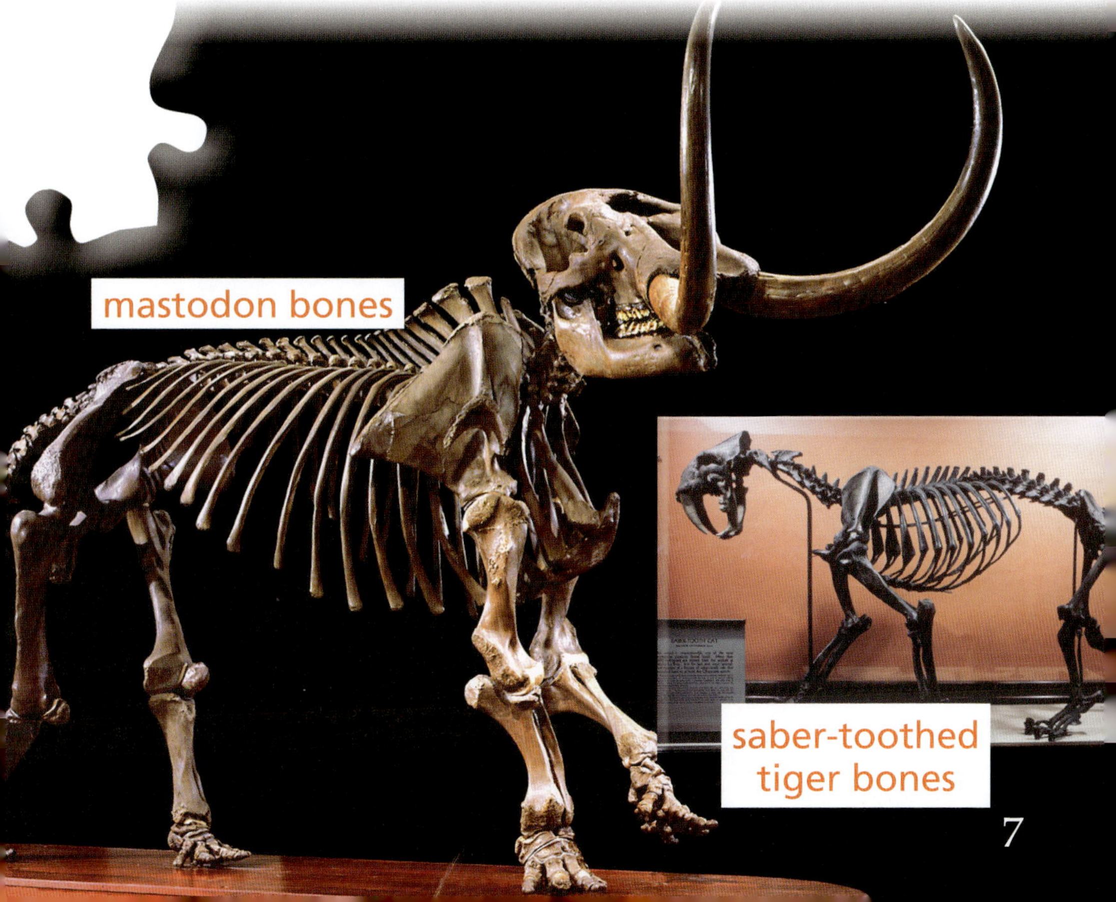

Clues in Ice

Scientists also find clues to the past in ice. There are places on Earth where the ice hardly ever melts. The ice acts like a freezer. It keeps dead animals' bodies from rotting.

Ice in this glacier might hold clues to the past.

This baby woolly mammoth looks like it just died. It's really over 40,000 years old!

Scientists have found whole woolly mammoths frozen in the ice. A woolly mammoth was a kind of elephant that lived many thousands of years ago.

Scientists have been uncovering the bodies of people in ice, too. In 1991, hikers in Europe discovered the body of a frozen man on a snow-covered mountain. The Ice Man had lived 5,000 years ago. He was still in some of his clothes and shoes!

This is where the Ice Man was found in the north of Italy.

Amber is like a beautiful stone and is used to make jewelry.

Clues in Amber

Scientists have found other kinds of clues in something called amber. Amber forms from sticky sap that drips out of trees. When the sap dries over many, many years, it gets hard and clear, like golden glass.

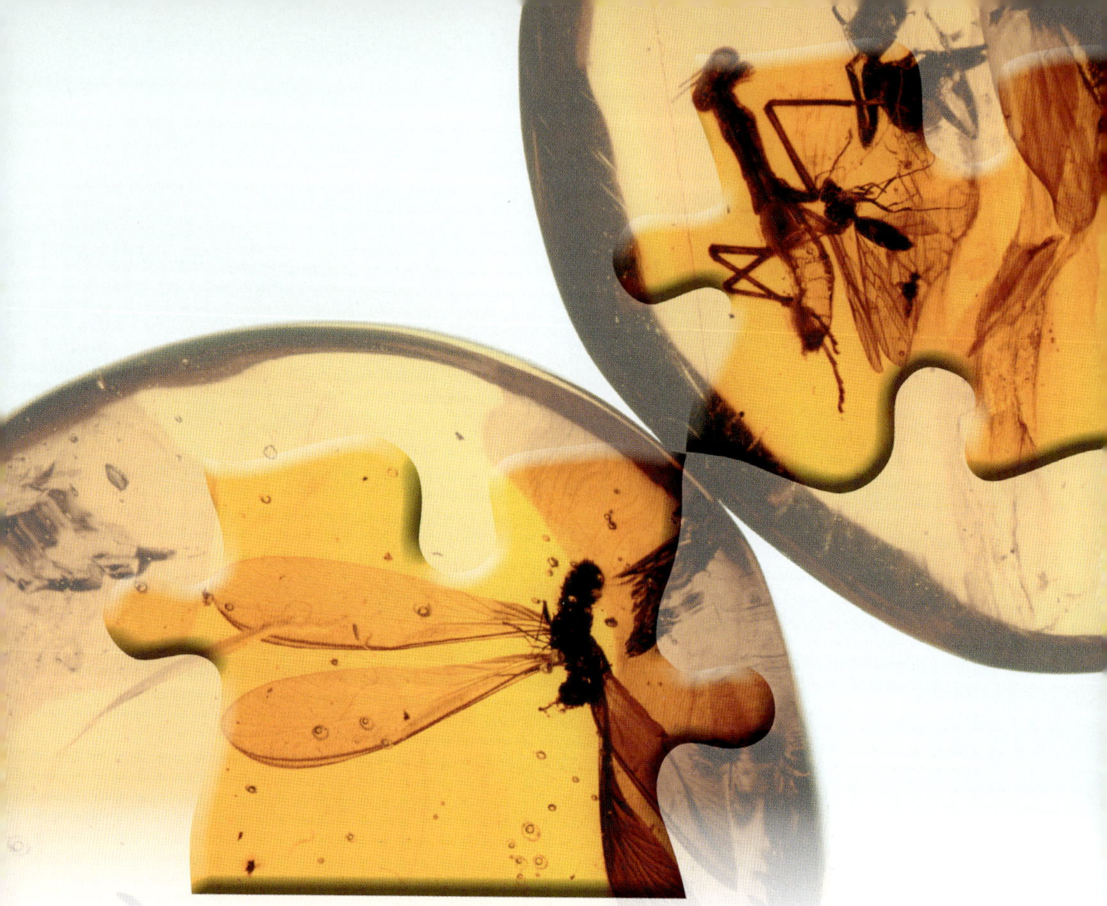

These insects in amber could be 90 million years old!

Millions of years ago, insects got stuck in sap. When the sap turned into hard amber, it kept the insects from rotting. Today, we can see exactly what these insects looked like.

What We Learn from Fossils

All of these clues are evidence that scientists study like detectives. They help scientists figure out what animals from long ago looked like.

Fossil bones are like pieces of a puzzle.

Fossil clues don't just prove that these animals lived long ago. They also tell a story about *how* these animals lived. An animal's teeth tell scientists what kinds of things an animal ate. An animal's feet tell scientists how it moved. Every part of an animal's body helps scientists unlock the secrets of life long ago.

Pointed teeth made this animal a good meat eater.

Responding

TARGET SKILL **Conclusions** Conclusions are smart guesses about a topic. Clues in the text help you make conclusions. Copy the chart below. Write two more text clues to complete the chart.

Text Clue	**Text Clue**	**Text Clue**
Fossils are found in the ground.	?	?

Conclusion Clues to the past can be found in many places.

Write About It

Text to Self Do you think it is interesting to learn about animals from long ago? Write a paragraph that gives your opinion. Tell why you think this.

TARGET VOCABULARY

buried	locations
clues	prove
evidence	remains
fierce	skeletons
fossils	uncovering

TARGET SKILL **Conclusions** Use details to figure out ideas that the author doesn't state.

TARGET STRATEGY **Visualize** As you read, use selection details to picture what is happening.

GENRE **Informational text** gives factual information about a topic.